T0128708

BREAKING THROUGH TO HIGHER PLACES

Nine Keys to Successful Fasting for Spiritual Breakthrough.

Diane Nethaway

authorHOUSE®

AuthorHouse™
1663 Liberty Drive
Bloomington, IN 47403
www.authorhouse.com
Phone: 1 (800) 839-8640

Published by AuthorHouse 12/22/2016

ISBN: 978-1-5246-5661-4 (sc)
ISBN: 978-1-5246-5659-1 (hc)
ISBN: 978-1-5246-5660-7 (e)

Library of Congress Control Number: 2016921117

Print information available on the last page.

DEDICATION

This book is dedicated first to my Lord and Savior who gave me the experience to write about.

Second, to my husband, Greg, who thought my experience was good enough to put into print and who encouraged me to write it.

Third, to my friends Brian and Sheryl Vallotton who opened up their cabin for me, so I could write without distraction and seek the Lord for an encounter.

Fourth, to my friend Shawn Lynch who did the very first edit of my book after it was first written.

And finally to my good friend Linda Heard who picked up an old copy I had and thought it was so good that not only did she encourage me to publish it, spend hours and hours of editing it, but with some friends of hers, Marilyn Sawya, Rob and Ali Simpson, created with a heart of obedience a publishing fund for me to work with.

I am so grateful for all the encouragement and support I have received.

CONTENTS

INTRODUCTION

My Story

Back in March of 2002, a local pastor asked me to teach a class on the Fruit of the Spirit at a prayer conference planned for May. I was thrilled, because I love teaching and encouraging women to grow in their walk with the Lord. I love going to a scripture passage and totally taking it apart and find some deeper truth I haven't seen before. I thought this subject would be just perfect since there were so many different avenues you could take with it. I had only spoken in front of a group of women twice before, and I loved every minute of it, so I was jumping out of my skin to do this until…

About a week or two later the pastor called me and told me she had changed my topic, and I would be teaching on fasting. I said, "Okay," but had this gigantic gulp in my throat and sheer panic was setting in. I had not practiced fasting consistently. How in the world was I going to be able to teach something that I myself hadn't done? How could I do this without feeling like the biggest hypocrite? I was about to pick up the phone and call her back, but the Lord spoke to my heart and said, "If you do this, I will teach you what you need to know." I wish I could say I immediately said, "Yes, Lord," but I can't. I had to chew on it for a couple of days before I was ready to trust and commit to His provision and promise.

I kept battling with my own selfish desires to get up and teach. I had dreams of speaking to different women's groups. This was my chance. Who could know when another opportunity was going to come my way? And this might just be a door opening for more speaking or teaching engagements in the future. But then, I had to deal with the fact that I couldn't successfully teach on something that I had not been doing in my own spiritual journey. I had to deal with my integrity issue and how guilty I would feel acting like I knew something I didn't. Sure, I did fast a couple of times, but usually it was a church thing, and I wasn't fully committed. And there was that one time…sigh.

Through my days of praying and trying to talk myself out of this, the Lord reminded me that the pastor who asked me to teach had called all the teachers, helpers, and speakers to a month-long fast. Every day we would pray for a specific teacher or speaker and follow the particular fast set for the day. I was still thinking, "How in the world is the Lord going to work this out?" but I decided to trust Him. I've always loved a good challenge. And besides what could it hurt?

The very first day of the fast and the eight days following it, God was true to His word and gave me one spiritual key to successful fasting for spiritual breakthrough for each day. It was amazing! I did not expect Him to move so fast, and what would take place in my own journey with Him would change my life forever.

CHAPTER ONE

Higher Places

*M*atthew *4:1-2 Then Jesus was led by the Spirit into the wilderness to be tempted there by the devil. For forty days and forty nights he fasted and became very hungry. (NLT)*

When Jesus was lead into the wilderness, He encountered temptations: three of those temptations which we are aware of dealt with **provision**, **power** and **protection** and came at the end of the 40 days. When we encounter these same things, it's usually with great frustration, anger and sometimes depression. If Jesus was tempted in the same ways we are, and He was able to conquer these temptations, how should this impact us? Your first thought might be, "Well, Jesus was God. He could do anything, and I am not Him." I have good news for you. Jesus tells us in *John 14:12, "I tell you the truth, anyone*

Diane Nethaway

who believes in me will do the same works I have done, and even greater works, because I am going to be with the Father."(NLT) This tells me that I can come out of the wilderness not only victorious, but there are endless possibilities of using those victories in ways that will be greater than the works of Jesus. Can you imagine what that would look like? I can't begin to understand what that would look like, but if God's word says it will happen, then I believe it. Just read the gospels of Matthew, Mark, Luke and John to see the things that Jesus did and ask yourself, "Am I doing these things today? What more could I or should I be doing?"

To understand and appreciate the victories, we must first understand the temptations. A temptation is defined as an enticement to do wrong by promise of pleasure or gain. (Merriam- Webster) God promises us in I Corinthians 10:13 that for every temptation there is a way out that is available and this will help us endure it. Jesus' way of enduring was to know the word of God and to speak it back to the Devil. (See Matthew 4) He was able to speak it back every time the enemy tried to use it against Him. The only way for us to quote scripture back in times of temptation is to know it!

The first temptation Jesus encountered is found in Matthew 4:3 *During that time the devil came and said to him, "If you are the Son of God, tell these stones to become loaves of bread."* (NLT) Satan came after Him in the area of **Provision**. In our own personal lives each

2

day, we are seeking ways to fulfill our own needs. We seek what we can feel, smell, hear, taste and see. But Jesus teaches us that those alone will not fill the void inside of us. God's word tells us to taste and see that the Lord is good, and if we seek Him first, all the things we truly need will be added to our lives. (Matthew 6:33 NKJV)

Jesus was hungry. He wasn't a little hungry. He was 40 days hungry. The Greek word **peinao** means famished. To be famished is to be extremely hungry. He had a need, and the Devil knew it. But Jesus tells him in *Matthew 4:4, "No! The Scriptures say, 'People do not live by bread alone, but by every word that comes from the mouth of God.'"* (NLT)

Jesus was referring to *Deuteronomy 8:2-7, 10 ²Remember how the Lord your God led you through the wilderness for these forty years, humbling you and testing you to prove your character, and to find out whether or not you would obey his commands.³ Yes, he humbled you by letting you go hungry and then feeding you with manna, a food previously unknown to you and your ancestors. He did it to teach you that people do not live by bread alone; rather, we live by every word that comes from the mouth of the* LORD. *⁴ For all these forty years your clothes didn't wear out, and your feet didn't blister or swell. ⁵ Think about it: Just as a parent disciplines a child, the Lord your God disciplines you for your own good. ⁶"So obey the commands of the Lord your God by walking in his ways and fearing him. ⁷ For the Lord your God is bringing you into a good land of flowing streams and pools of water, with fountains and springs that gush out in the valleys and hills...* [10] *When you have eaten your fill, be sure to praise the* LORD *your God for the good land he has given you.* (NLT)

The wilderness is a time for humbling, the proving of our character and to test our faith and endurance in obeying what He tells us to do. When we enter our own wilderness experience while fasting, our hunger reminds us that we can eat all the food in the world, but it will never fill the real hunger which is for the Lord. We discover who He is, and how great His love is for us when we spend time reading, praying, and waiting for Him to respond back. Jesus knew the Word and was able to quote it in times of trouble when the enemy came at Him in His physical weakness, and He was able to remain strong. When the enemy uses provision as a temptation in your life, knowing the word of God will also make you strong.

Just recently our landlords informed us they are going to sell the house we are living in. My heart sank when I heard that because every two to three years this has been happening to us. Prior to this information, Greg and I had read a book by Francis Chan called *Crazy Love.* The book impacted us so much that we decided the next time we moved, we would downsize so that we were not living paycheck to paycheck to pay our rent, but we could use the extra money to help our family and other people in need.

Two weeks after we got that notice, Greg got a call from a friend who wanted him to go look at a house he saw in the paper that was for rent. Greg couldn't believe what he saw and called me and said, "You've got to see this house. It's amazing and you are going to fall in love with it. The only problem is its $100 more than what we are paying now." I remembered our declaration but decided I wanted to see it anyway.

A few hours later I was standing in front of the most beautifully landscaped piece of land that I had ever seen. The house sat on two acres. There was an area behind the house that could have easily been a baseball field and behind that was a place to build bonfires. They had been using this for their youth group on several occasions. Directly behind that was a horse corral that the son was using for paintball games. The inside was beautiful too but I could care less what it looked like on the inside. I was looking at the land and seeing everything I had been praying for, for the last 20 years. The front yard had a pond with running water that was heaven to my ears. The kitchen had a patio surrounded by tons of greenery and was a great place to get up in the mornings and have my devotions. My mouth was salivating. The pool was enclosed and the master bedroom opened up to it as well as a beautiful Jacuzzi. I was dying inside and everything in my flesh was saying, "Take it! This is what you have been praying for." I didn't have peace though because of our declaration to downsize. The people renting the house wanted us to take the house so badly but Greg and I told them we would have to pray about it first.

The upcoming weekend was our 6th Biannual 24 Hour Prayer Focus. We told them we would let them know at the end of it. Our intention was not to tell anyone, but sometime during the Prayer Focus we would have some good friends pray for us and see what God would speak to them for us. We didn't get that opportunity because there were lines for prayer and our friends had to leave before we could get in there.

It was an hour and a half before the service started and we still didn't have an answer so we sought out one of the prayer intercessors that was still there. We asked him to pray for us and see what the Lord would impress on him. After a few minutes he tells Greg, "Do whatever the woman tells you to do." I was saying, "No! No! Don't lay that on me." I was feeling so weak and didn't want to get the blame for the sin I wanted to commit. I wanted Greg to. If he made the decision, I didn't have to reap what **I** had sown but we would reap what **he** had sown. Eve wasn't going to get the blame this time: Adam would. (See Genesis 3) How silly of me because in all rationality, we would have both reaped what **he** had done.

Greg decided to run home and change clothes. I went to my office crying out to God for an answer that would be specific and that I would have peace. Meanwhile the man who prayed for us was up at the altar praying, then came back and says to me, "It's a test!" My heart sank. "No! Really? That means I can't have the house, doesn't it?" He just stood there and said again, "It's a test." I took a breath and said, "Okay. I can release this then." As soon as I said that a peace came over me, and I knew we were making the right decision. I called Greg and told him it was a test, and then he too felt that peace. We let the house go trusting and believing that God would lead us to the right home at the right time.

I can't imagine the misery we would have felt later if we had been in a hurry to get what we wanted. Knowing God's word and that He would supply all our needs and understanding how the enemy was using the temptation of provision, kept us from making a very big mistake.

The second temptation Jesus encountered was the need for **Protection**. *Matthew 4:5-6 ⁵Then the devil took him to the holy city, Jerusalem, to the highest point of the Temple, ⁶ and said, "If you are the Son of God, jump off! For the Scriptures say, 'He will order his angels to protect you. And they will hold you up with their hands so you won't even hurt your foot on a stone.'"* (NLT) I think there are times that we have the attitude that everything will work out and that God will protect us when we make bad choices, so we get careless and jump into things we should have never been involved with. We know what's right and wrong, but in order to satisfy our own desires, we cast our cares to the wind. The Word clearly tells us we will reap what we sow. Although God forgives us when we ask, the consequences still have to be dealt with and learned from. We need to understand that our sin does not just affect us, but it affects everyone around us and those who are in our sphere of influence. We need to stop being in a hurry and trust that God's timing is perfect, and He will do what He says. *Proverbs 30:5 Every word of God proves true. He is a shield to all who come to him for protection.* (NLT) God is our shield of protection and if we walk out in front of that shield, we walk right into the schemes and lies of the enemy. ***When we believe the lie, we empower the lie.***

Jesus again quotes scripture back, *Matthew 4:7 Jesus responded, "The Scriptures also say, 'You must not test the Lord your God.'"* (NLT) Here He was referring to *Deuteronomy 6:16 You must not test the Lord your God as you did when you complained at Massah.* (NLT) We find the story of Massah in Exodus 17:1-7. After seeing all the miracles that God had done for them, they arrived at a place where they were out of water. Instead of being faithful and trusting God to provide, they started grumbling and saying, "Is the Lord among us or not?" How many times have we asked that same question when things didn't happen as fast as we wanted them to or the way we wanted them to? They were not only questioning God's presence but His choice of leadership.

In our quest to fulfill our desires, we often forget about what God has already done in the past. We start grumbling and complaining and often questioning if God really cares for us. We make bad choices and then when consequences happen, we get mad at God because He doesn't bail us out. We start growing angry at those whom God has put in leadership. We start blaming the church. I have seen this happen over and over. When someone in leadership or a member of the body has offended someone in the church, they leave the church. They forget the church body as a whole has walked with them through life, death, weddings, graduations, fun times and bad times. They leave mad at leadership and the offender without even trying to work it out. They leave mad at a person or persons, and think they are only leaving them, not recognizing they are leaving their whole church family. One thing makes them mad and all of a sudden they forget all the good things their church family has walked through with them in the past. It's so sad! We also get mad at our closest friends, and many times we blame our childhood. The truth is we don't blame the true source of our problem: ourselves. God in His mercy will sometimes give us a lot of grace over these situations and eventually gives us what we want, but then we forget all about it and move on to more times of grumbling.

The third temptation dealt with **Power.** *Matthew 4:8-9* [8] *Next the devil took him to the peak of a very high mountain and showed him all* *the kingdoms of the world and their glory. ⁹ "I will give it all to you," he*

said, "if you will kneel down and worship me." (NLT)

The definition of power is possession of control, authority, or influence over someone or something. (Merriam-Webster) The Devil was temping Jesus to forgo the suffering and the cross by giving Him the rulership of the nations now. Why should He have to wait for what is already rightfully His? His plan was to draw Jesus away from the plan of redemption by enticing Him to grab the kingdom the Father had promised to give Him. Instead of enduring the long, bitter, and painful road to the cross, He could rule the world now. The devil was trying to entice Him to skip ahead of the plan.

Life works the same way: we don't get a promotion to the next level until we learn the basics. It's important to keep the goal before us. We need to press on to reach the end of the race and receive the heavenly prize for which God, through Christ Jesus, is calling us. (See Philippians 3:14)

God wants us to have clear revelations of His plans for us. He has great plans to prosper us and not to hurt us. He wants to give us a hope and a future, and when we pray, He will hear us. He says if we look to Him wholeheartedly, we will find Him. He goes on to tell us that He will release us from our captivity whether it comes in the form of temptations, addiction or complacency. (See Jeremiah 29:11-14)

Life is like going through school. You have preschool, kindergarten, elementary, high school and college. No one goes from preschool to college. The goal is college, but to get there we have to learn the lessons taught in the former levels of schooling, and we have to take the tests to pass. If we go to college before we have learned the fundamentals, we would likely fail every class, never be prepared for the tests or just get by, and although we are at college there will be no clear vision of what to do next. We can't skip ahead of the plan.

We often think that we shouldn't have pain in the journey. But it's the comfort that comes after the pain that helps us see that it was all worth it. It made us wiser and stronger. Jesus needed to go through the wilderness. He needed to overcome the temptations He faced in order for His ministry to be effective. Because He went through suffering and testing, He is able to help us when we are tempted and show us how to overcome our temptations. We see later in the passage that Jesus walks by two brothers and says "Follow me," and they both drop what they are doing, no questions asked, and follow Him. They saw something in Him. I would like to say it was a strength they in themselves didn't have, and it drew them into His ministry. When we go through our own wildernesses not giving up but facing them and growing from them, and as we overcome and gain strength, people will want to follow us into our ministries too.

Jesus responded to Satan with *Matthew 4:10 "Get out of here, Satan," Jesus told him. "For the Scriptures say, 'You must worship the Lord your God and serve only him.'"* Jesus was referring to *Deuteronomy 6:13 You must fear the* LORD *your God and serve him. When you take an oath, you must use only his name.* (NLT) Satan tempted Jesus with what seemed like the easy way and wanted Him to prostrate Himself and revere him and him only. When the Israelites were moving into the Promised Land, the Lord warned them not to worship the idols or gods of their neighbors. He knew if they started allowing these things into their lives, they would forget Him, and it would destroy their lives. He told them that the Lord their God who lived among them was a jealous God. We are told both in Deuteronomy and the Gospels that we are to love the Lord with all our heart, soul and our strength: not part. The enemy still comes at us today with temptations of idol worship in the form of material possessions, addictions, and self-gratification. **Whatever we spend time worshipping, we give power to.** When we fast and pray, we too will come to a place where we either trust God to provide for us, or we continue to do things the old way: satisfying the desire of our flesh with temporary fixes.

There are no easily traveled roads. Many of us have tried to take the wide road because it looked like it offered more, but we eventually find ourselves disillusioned by what we find. Although it gave us temporary satisfaction and possibly a few thrills here and there, we eventually find ourselves at another fork in the road and still trying to figure out where to go next. A lot of the time we end up taking the fork in the road that leads back to where we started from. The narrow road keeps us more focused and less distracted. Although we have the choice to take the wide road at any time, we have a better view of where we are going and how to get to our destination on the narrow road.

Since Jesus was led by the Spirit into the wilderness, and the Word says that He fasted for 40 days, fasting had to be a vital part of the wilderness journey. Fasting throughout the pages of the Bible was practiced for protection, intimacy, insight into God's plans, increase of power in ministry, instruction, seeking direction, answers to prayers, victory in times of spiritual warfare, and to soften hearts. Just as it does today.

Fasting and praying gives us opportunity to remember where we have been and where we are today. For me, I often will take a journey back through my journal, reminisce, and find great joy in the person I am becoming, and how much I've matured. I see visions and promises that are yet to be fulfilled, and it encourages me to push forward and not give up and to keep growing. There are places in those journals that I just want to kick myself for complaining instead of trusting. I recognize there is still so much more for me to learn. I don't have to put God to the test. I don't have to ask if He is with me. I press forward **recognizing** that I haven't achieved all that God has for me, I am running a race that I intend to finish: a race that He has planned out for me, and there is a prize at the end of it! My journals have become a time-line where I can see markers where God has moved in my life and the turning points where growth and maturity took place.

Fasting and praying helps us recognize the illusion of temporary satisfaction in things rather than the complete satisfaction we can find in the Lord. We live in a world of instant gratification. Fasting shifts our desires from satisfying the flesh to desiring more spiritual things and gives us more understanding of our identity. We are made in the image of God. We are his sons and daughters. We've been adopted as heirs. *Galatians 3:29 And now that you belong to Christ, you are the true children of Abraham. You are his heirs, and God's promise to Abraham belongs to you.* (NLT) We are His bride and He is coming back to get us. ***Fasting changes our hearts from wanting our way to wanting His.***

When Jesus was led into the wilderness, it was by the Spirit. It was intentional. The word led is the Greek word **anago,** which means He was led up. To be led up is to be led in a more elevated position, as to climb to the top of a ladder. The wilderness is the higher place. We often enter the wilderness crying, angry, and with great dread thinking that this is the lowest form of punishment and testing. We start asking God, "Why me?" or "Why are You doing this to me?" I wonder what would happen if we started entering it with joy, great expectation, and started believing that God is going to meet us there. Yes, we will be tempted, but Jesus already went through it, will help us, and He knows how to tug on the strings of the Father's heart.

Every wilderness experience is an opportunity for change and a deeper intimacy with God. Can you think back to a time when you said you wanted to be like Jesus? Can you remember asking him to help you to treat people the way Jesus would have? Have you asked God for a deeper more intimate relationship with Him?

Well, be careful of what you ask for because going through the wilderness will reveal who you really are. But then, when you see the truth and acknowledge it, God can release you from your captivity, the kind of captivity that keeps you from growing and deepening your relationship with Him.

Jesus didn't eat during His wilderness experience. He knew the importance of fasting. I am convinced that fasting in the wilderness will open doors for us to walk in power because we will be full of the Spirit. When Jesus referred to the Scriptures in Deuteronomy, there was a promise of reward and a warning. The promise was that God would take them into a good land where food was plentiful and nothing was lacking, their enemies would be driven away, and

God would multiply what they had. God still does that today. The good land is the place God sends us to fulfill the calling of our life ministries. God still supplies all of our needs from His glorious riches which have been given to us in Jesus. (See Philippians 4:19) And if we humble ourselves and resist the devil, he will flee.`

The warning is not to become proud and forget the Lord. Don't forget where He has led you so far. Remember the Lord, because it is He who gives you the power to be successful. When the Lord revealed to us that we couldn't have my dream house, I could have gotten very angry at God for "teasing" me. But I chose to remember where He had already brought us from. We lived in the tiniest house in Fremont, California. When we moved to Tracy, California, we got a new home that was 1600 square feet. To me that was a mansion. After living there for eight years, God moved us again and every two to three years after that. Every home He provided was greater than the house before. I still can't believe the wonderful home we are living in now has been ours for almost three years. I remain in that place of gratitude! God will take me to the place He wants me and my family to be in and I WANT to be where He is.

If we forget, His word says we will be destroyed. This can come in many forms, from ministries failing to physical death. He knows when we walk away from Him to serve false idols, the enemy is victorious, and it is he who prowls as a lion ready to devour those who don't stay alert. (See I Peter 5:8)

In Luke 4:1 Jesus came into the wilderness **full** of the Spirit, and in Luke 4:14 it says Jesus returned back to Galilee in the **power** of the Spirit. *Matthew 4:11 Then the devil went away, and angels came and took care of Jesus.* And in *Matthew 4:17 From then on Jesus began to preach, "Repent of your sins and turn to God, for the Kingdom of Heaven is near."* (NLT) We are told in *I Peter 5:10 In his kindness God called you to share in his eternal glory by means of Christ Jesus. So after you have suffered a little while he will restore, support and strengthen you and he will place you on a firm foundation!* (NLT) We too can be led into the wilderness by the Spirit to higher places, and after we have suffered a little, we will stand on a much firmer foundation in our faith. Our faith will lead us to do things we could never have done prior to our wilderness experience. Jesus told His disciples in Matthew 21:21-23 that if we have faith and don't doubt, we can do things like making a fig tree shrivel or telling a mountain to be lifted and thrown into the sea. When something in our life isn't bearing fruit like that fig tree Jesus saw on the way to Jerusalem, (See Matthew 21:18-19) or we are facing mountains in the form of adversities, our faith can move them out of our way. When they are moved out of the way or destroyed, we will come out of the wilderness experience restored, supported and strengthened, or we can choose to come out defeated because we couldn't see the beauty in the wilderness. It's all about how we **choose** to view it.

I've been through a lot of wilderness experiences and have found God to be true to the lessons He taught me. We will be tempted with provision, protection and power but just like Jesus we can overcome them and walk in the power of the Spirit and renewed faith.

Questions to Ponder from Chapter One

1. What is your definition of temptation?

2. What was the last temptation you faced and how did you handle it?

3. Read Psalm 119:11. How can knowing God's word keep you from falling into temptation?

4. Can you think of a time when you were tempted to do something and a verse or scripture popped into your head? What was the scripture?

5. Read I Corinthians 10:12-13. What does this scripture tell us about our attitude and how we should view temptations?

6. Think back to a time you were really hungry. How did it make you feel?

7. How do you know the difference between true hunger for food and hunger that wants to fill an emotional need?

8. Next time you feel hungry ask yourself, "Do I need to feed my stomach or my soul?

9. Have you ever complained to God asking Him, "Why are you doing this to me?"

10. Looking back now, can you see the real reason you were where you were when you asked the question? What do you think that was?

11. Do you take risks that you shouldn't expecting God to bail you out or protect you? What was the most recent risk you have taken?

12. Can you think of a time when you didn't wait on God and tried to make something happen before it was time? What was it?

13. What did you learn from it and how can you apply it to your life today?

14. What was the last wilderness experience you faced? Was it in the area of provision, power or protection?

15. What did the last wilderness experience teach you? How did it affect who you are today?

16. If you didn't fast through that time, what would have been the benefits of fasting during that wilderness experience? How could it have changed your life?

17. Take a few moments and write down at least 10 things that God has done for you.

18. Why is it important not to forget the good things that God has done for you?

19. happens when we become ungrateful?

20. How does it affect our home life? Work place? Church relationships?

21. How have wilderness experiences increased your faith? Can you see the wilderness as a "Higher place"? How do you think you will handle the next one?

CHAPTER TWO

What Is Fasting?

F asting is making a choice to abstain from food to accomplish a particular purpose directed by God or a denying of ourselves things that keep us distracted from God, so we can seek after His heart and His revelations. In the same way that eating strengthens our physical life, fasting strengthens our spiritual life.

A successful fast accomplishes several things. It reveals how much the flesh has power over our thought life and emotions. It functions as a way to break the flesh's hold on our spirit. And it draws us into a deeper more intimate relationship with the Lord as He reveals more of Himself to us.

In the book of Isaiah, chapter 58 shows us many rewards of fasting. It:

1. Frees us from the things that bind us

2. Lightens our burdens

3. Sets us free from the things that burden us down

4. Breaks the chains of addictions

5. Reminds us to give to the poor and needy

6. Reminds us to take care of family

7. Enlightens us and brings clarity to our situations

8. Brings healings quickly

9. Helps us walk in a morally upright way which will be noticed by others

10. Brings the fullness of God to protect us from surprise attacks: keeps us alert

11. Brings answers to prayer

12. Brings happiness out of misery

13. Gives light in times of misfortune

14. Brings guidance from the Lord

15. Brings refreshing in dry times

16. Restores strength

17. Allows for thriving and flourishing in hard times

18. Brings restoration

19. Brings the power of God into our ministry

The Greek word for fasting **Nesteou** means not to eat and, the Hebrew word for fasting **Tsuwm** means to cover over the mouth. Although you may hear of several types of fasts ranging from not watching TV to eliminating something from your daily activity, I have found personally for me that it's the growl of the tummy or the denial of the craving that reminds me that my emptiness can only be filled by God our Father.

The whole purpose of the fast is to empty ourselves in order to point our thoughts to God, His revelations of love for us and doing His will. Hunger reminds us that we are empty or missing something which reveals to us our need for God and encourages intimacy with Him. It helps us tune in to God when we get too busy for Him. It's kind of like a TV on a channel that has a jumbled picture or a radio that has a static sound. We can't see clearly what is happening and we can't understand what is being said, and if we do hear anything, it's a couple of words here and there. In order to see or hear better, we have to change it to a better channel. Fasting is the way to bring a clear picture to us or clear up the static in our lives and minds, so we can see and hear God better.

Fasting before the Lord is actually feasting with Him. *Revelation 3:20 Behold, I stand at the door and knock; if anyone hears My voice and opens the door, I will come in to him and will dine with him, and he with Me.* (NASB) We have an opportunity through fasting to engage with the Lord and to hang on to every word He speaks to us. He said He would dine with us. Usually when we take a meal together as a family, we talk about our day and share our thoughts. Can you picture yourself sitting at a table with the King of Kings and Lord of Lords just talking about the day together? Our meal during fasting becomes the Word, our conversation is our prayer and our meditation is our seeking.

Fasting becomes the key to unlock doors to areas in our life where other keys have failed. Keys can fit into a lock and seem for one second to be the right one until you try to turn it. Unfortunately some of us go through many keys until we find the right one. We won't be able to unlock those areas until we find the right key.

We allow so many things into our lives which seem to fit, but once we engage them, we soon realize it wasn't the right thing. For me that came into play with ministry. Every time there would be a need mentioned, and no one stepped up to the plate; "Super Diane" came to the rescue. I figured the key to getting things done was to do it myself. I would get so depressed when what I was doing would not turn into something successful. No one would show up. No one would offer to help. No one seemed to care and most of the time the one who came to me, pointing out the need, was the one least interested. Depression led me to pouting and pulling out of everything, to being angry at everyone for not supporting me. Today when someone comes to me and says we should have this or that in the church, I tell them, "Since you feel this way, it may mean you need to pray about it, and see how God wants _you_ to make it happen." If I get an inclination to do something now, and am not sure whether it's my need to fix everything or it's a true call from God, I know that fasting will open the door to clarity and revelation from God.

Fasting and prayers are the keys for unlocking the deep things of God. Once those doors are opened the possibilities are endless. We voluntarily abstain from food in order to accomplish a God-directed purpose or we deny ourselves things that keep us from focusing on God's heart and His revelations. With a clear mind we can then take the path that He has designed for us with confidence and expectation.

This book is not about what kind of fasts you can choose to go on because I find it's better if that's between you and God. It will be about how you can find successful spiritual breakthrough through fasting.

In March of 2002, the Lord took me on a fasting journey in which He gave me Nine Keys to Successful Fasting for Spiritual Breakthrough. The rest of this book is dedicated to those Nine Keys.

Questions to Ponder from Chapter Two

1. What have you been taught about fasting in the past?

2. How have you seen others fast and how did it shape your perception of fasting?

3. When was the last time you fasted?

4. Was it a successful fast? What made the fast successful for you?

5. Have you ever had an unsuccessful fast? What caused the fast to fail?

6. In Isaiah 58 there are several rewards from fasting. Which of these rewards are areas that still need improvement or breakthrough in your life?

7. What types of things have you fasted, and why did you choose that particular fast?

8. How did the Lord show up in this/these fasts?

9. Is there something in your life that you are seeking an answer for that you feel could be found through fasting?

10. Read Judges 20:26-29. What can we learn about fasting from these verses?

11. What are the things today that are keeping you from fasting?

CHAPTER THREE

The first key to successful fasting for spiritual breakthrough: Go into fasting wholeheartedly and with an attitude of expectation.

Fasting Day One

The first thing I noticed, on my first day, was this fast was all about attitude. I was going into this fast with an attitude of expectation for a spiritual breakthrough. My prayer was that God would keep the excitement going. I had to look at my former fasting occasions with honesty and came to the conclusion that I was only going through the motions because it was the right thing to do, or someone told me I had to do it. I also realized I had a "ho hum" attitude.

A week before we did this "official prayer conference fast", I had fasted on a Wednesday prior to the event. I don't remember the reason why, but I did remember how God had opened up so many truths to me that I almost had to say, "Stop! Lord you are giving me too much and I can't handle it all." God was already preparing me and enticing me to join Him on this journey, and I didn't even know it.

The first scripture He gave me on my first day of fasting was *Psalm 103:1 Let all that I am praise the Lord; with my whole heart, I will praise his holy name.* (NLT) He was showing me that I couldn't be thinking about lunch and praising Him at the same time. He deserved my whole heart, not just a portion. I needed to be doing this fast for the right reasons. I didn't want to honor Him with just my lips, and yet have my heart far away from Him. (See Isaiah 9:13) I wanted to worship Him because He was worth it, not because someone told me to do it.

Psalm 103:2 Let all that I am praise the Lord; may I never forget the good things he does for me. (NLT) I praise the Lord not only for what He has done *for* me, but I praise Him *all the time* even when I feel He hasn't done anything new. I make sure not to forget the good things and try to recognize that what He doesn't do is just as important and praiseworthy. It's a combination of the two not a separation. I know as I trust in the Lord, I will never lack any good thing. It would become a very important thing to do this in those thirty days especially because

I was denying my flesh to focus on the good things. My Father was not going to withhold any good thing from me as I focused on doing what was right.

When we fast, our whole focus should be on the Father and drawing near to His heart. We start by being thankful and praising him. Praise puts us in His presence. In His presence we find strength and joy. Then, wait quietly before Him and give Him the chance to speak. It's not that He never speaks, but our minds are so full of what's going on in our lives, that we don't take the time to just sit and hear what He has to say. We think when we pray, it means we do all the talking, and when we get done we don't linger to hear His answers. *Psalm 62:5 Let all that I am wait quietly before God, for my hope is in him.* (NLT)

When we go into fasting with an attitude of expectation and wholeheartedly, we should **expect a manifested awareness of God's presence**. *John 14:21 Those who accept my commandments and obey them are the ones who love me. And because they love me, my Father will love them. And I will love them and reveal myself to each of them* (NLT) When our focus is off food, or whatever takes up our time, we spend more time thinking about God and loving Him, and He makes His presence known to us. We gain fresh new insights and therefore increase in discernment. Confidence and faith in God is strengthened, and we find mental, spiritual and physical refreshment.

Many times before going into a fast, **expect to be called to it**. We need to be called to a fast just as we are called to ministry and go into it wholeheartedly. We need to be careful not to miss the times He calls us. There will be times that we ourselves will want fresh revelation and intimacy and choose to go on a fast. There are also times when the Church is being called to a corporate fast. Even with these, we need to seek God's counsel. We need to be careful not to go into a fast for the wrong reasons, such as "It's the thing to do", to lose weight or because someone tells you to. If we fast for the wrong reason, it will affect our heart, make us powerless and will bear no fruit. If we go into fasting with the wrong motive, it will become drudgery, legalism, and something we could eventually despise.

We must go into fasting **expecting answers to prayer.** *Isaiah 58:9 Then when you call, the Lord will answer. 'Yes, I am here,' he will quickly reply...* (NLT) He tells us to seek, and we will find, ask and it will be given to us, to knock and He will open the door. (See Matthew 7:7) When I am fasting, I am seeking Him wholeheartedly, asking Him to hear my prayer just like a child asks for something from her father, and I am knocking for the doors to be opened to spiritual enlightenment and direction for my life or the lives of the ones I am praying for.

And finally as we fast, we should **expect a spiritual breakthrough**. When the Spirit is in control, He will drag the rest of our body along.

Galatians 5:16-18, 22-23 [16]*So I say, let the Holy Spirit guide your lives. Then you won't be doing what your sinful nature craves.* [17] *The sinful nature wants to do evil, which is just the opposite of what the Spirit wants. And the Spirit gives us desires that are the opposite of what the sinful nature desires. These two forces are constantly fighting each other, so you are not free to carry out your good intentions.* [18] *But when you are directed by the Spirit, you are not under obligation to the law of Moses...* [22] *But the Holy Spirit produces this kind of fruit in our lives: love, joy, peace, patience, kindness, goodness, faithfulness,* [23] *gentleness, and self-control. There is no law against these things!* (NLT)

Fasting for spiritual breakthrough involves having a wholehearted expectancy that God will meet with us, reveal Himself to us and answer our prayers.

Questions to Ponder from Chapter Three

1. Read Judges 20:26-29. What can we learn about fasting from these verses?

2. What are the things today that are keeping you from fasting?

3. If you were going on a fast today, considering where you are in your relationship with God, what would your expectation be?

4. What expectations can we have while fasting?

5. Can you think of a time when you were in the Word and you had to ask God to slow down, because you were getting an overload of information from Him? What was He showing you?

6. When you spend time with the Lord, how much time would you say that you give to waiting silently for Him to answer?

7. What is it that keeps you from sitting quietly before the Lord? What are some changes you could make in your life to make this possible?

8. How would you describe your private worship experience with the Lord? In Church?

9. What is the most recent insight the Lord has given you from His word?

CHAPTER FOUR

The second key to successful fasting for spiritual breakthrough: **Know your purpose and what type of fast you are going to do. Make a plan!!!!**

Fasting Day Two

My second day I felt a bit weak. I prayed that God would be my strength. My first day was a lot easier than I thought it would be. God had reminded me of a dream the day before I started the fast that confirmed to me that this fast would not only be for the women at the conference, but it was going to be for my own personal life.

The scripture the Lord led me to for this day was *Psalm 1:1-3 ¹Oh, the joys of those who do not follow the advice of the*

wicked, or stand around with sinners, or join in with mockers.
² But they delight in the law of the Lord, meditating on it day and
night ³ They are like trees planted along the riverbank, bearing fruit
each season. Their leaves never wither, and they prosper in all they
do. (NLT)

As soon as we know our purpose, we will not be in danger of playing it "by ear". We delight in doing it God's way not our flesh's way. We can fast any way we choose. The method doesn't matter as much as the motivation behind it. The flesh will deceive us into thinking we are too weak or we must have a bite of_____. So we substitute what wasn't planned to give in to the flesh. People will try to deceive us and say, "Well, you'd better be careful and not over-do it," or "It's ok to have just one bite". Satan did the same thing to Eve in the Garden of Eden. (See Genesis 3:3-5) If we are called to it, God will be our strength, and He never gives us more than we can handle. If we commit them to the Lord, our plans will succeed.

When we make a plan and stick to it, then we are free to spend time with the Lord without things getting in the way. Not that there aren't times when that will happen, but they will happen less and less, and we will find ourselves having more time than we thought possible. The list of excuses starts to run out, because we are so fired up to spend time with the Lord. The more time we spend with God in fellowship, worship and adoration of Him, and the more we read

His word, the greater our effectiveness will be in prayer, the greater the desire to sit at His feet becomes, and the more meaningful this fast will be.

Our times of fasting should result in bearing fruit and not becoming weak. According to Galatians 5:22 the fruit we are hoping to produce in our lives are love, joy, peace, patience, kindness, goodness, faithfulness, gentleness, and self control. The plan is to allow this fruit to replace the desires or habits of our old, dead, crucified, sinful nature. My expectation is spiritual breakthrough in these areas for myself and to use them to impact others. Times will get hard, but as we stand firm and press forward, God will help us follow the steps that will bring good fruit. The hard times are actually pruning us, so we can bear the good fruit and keep bearing it. As we go through fasting, the messages we receive should cause us to remain in Christ, and become more receptive to the work He is doing in us. The good fruit will be harvested and bring great enjoyment to those who are partaking of it. And when fruit tastes good, they keep coming back for more. So not only is change taking place in our lives, it is also taking place in the heart of those in our sphere of influence.

My plan was to fast for 30 days, read the Bible, take notes on what I would learn each day, apply it to my life and then teach it to others. When you decide on which fast you will do, plan it out. For instance, you might choose to do a Daniel Fast. Determine how many days you will fast, and what you will eat, and when you will eat. It's important you also plan to spend time each day in the Word and prayer, so you can receive instruction. Also plan how you will *come off the fast.* Plus you will need to plan how you will handle certain events or situations that will put you in places where meals are going to be served. Once your plan is in place, you are less likely to veer off it.

Should you go off your fast, ask God for forgiveness, receive it and restart right where you are. The enemy will use condemnation and guilt to keep you from continuing. You might start thinking that God will punish you and not speak, but God knows the intent of the heart. He will not condemn you, and I believe He is thrilled when you get right back up and keep seeking Him. I also believe He will give you the breakthrough you desire. He knows the enemy is going to try to tempt you. I think it's a personal victory for you when you overcome, but as you continue from the fall, God will still honor your attempt.

Know your purpose and make a plan then watch and see how God directs your path.

Questions to Ponder from Chapter Four

1. Read Galatians 5:19-21. What are the desires of the flesh?

2. Read Galatians 5:22-23.What is the fruit of the Spirit? What happens to the good fruit produced in our lives?

3. What does Roman 6:5-6 tell us about sin?

4. Have there been times in your life when you could see sin losing its power? What made that change happen?

5. What should you do if your plan fails and you go off your fast?

6. What are some things the enemy might use to make you go off your plan or give up?

7. Let's pretend you are going on a fast this coming Monday. Take a few moments and write out your plan.

    a.   What type of fast will you do?

    b. If you are eating anything, what will those things be?

    c. How long will you be on your fast?

    d. What will you do when you get hungry?

    e. When will you spend time in the Word?

    f. What events are coming up that could be a hindrance to your plan?

    g. Write down how you will handle each of them.

h. How will you handle your fast at meal times for those in your family who aren't fasting with you?

i. Name at least three people you can make yourself accountable to, to help you succeed.

CHAPTER FIVE

The third key to successful fasting for spiritual breakthrough: **Pray, Read His word, Journal what He tells you, and Be satisfied with the meal He provides.**

Fasting Day Three

T he second night of my fast was extremely hard as the hunger pangs were strong, and I couldn't sleep. It was a relief when I made it through the night. As morning drew near I realized, my excitement and expectations were growing higher each day. I had a sense of feeling clean and crisp and of God's hands touching my life. And this was only the third day. My brain felt clear and ready to receive whatever God wanted to speak or show me.

Pray! It was through a dream about an upcoming attack that the Lord spoke to my heart about getting intercessors to pray for me. As I prayed, He began to show me their faces. I was beginning to see that I was at the beginning of one incredible journey. Scriptures about paths kept jumping off the pages in my Bible.

One of the most effective ways to pray is to pray the scriptures. I love reading His word and writing my prayers out to reflect what He gives me for the day. Sometimes when I go back and read them, I can't believe those prayers came from me. Following is an excerpt from my prayer journal after reading Song of Solomon Chapter One.

"Oh God, we know you as Father, Creator, the Omnipotent One. Holy Spirit we know you as Comforter, Counselor, Convictor of Sin and Illuminator of the Word. Jesus we know you as Savior, Lord, King of Kings and Friend. But what I am coming to know now is a large percentage of us really don't know you as Lover: Lover of our Souls.

Song of Solomon says, **"Kiss me with the kisses of your mouth for your love is better than wine."** *This should be the cry of your church: a bride to her bridegroom. A kiss is a seal that we are now in an intimate relationship with you. A kiss leaves us in anticipation of the knowledge, that there is more to come. A kiss is an indication that we have moved from knowing about you to knowing you more intimately. This knowledge should leave us in anticipation of what is coming, and this is far better than what wine represents: worldly pleasures. Father,* *help us get to that place, where we are asking you to kiss us with the kisses of your mouth. Let your words draw us deeper. Let us become that bride who is all dressed in white, who has saved herself for the wedding day that is to come. Help us have that passionate awareness and excitement, as we begin our walk down the aisle to you.*

For the men of the church help them to understand how the excitement and anticipation that they have or will have as they see their bride walking toward them is the same feeling you have toward them."

Fasting without praying is like eating without swallowing. When Daniel started praying, it took twenty-one days for the answer to come. The angel told him *"...since the first day you began to pray for understanding and to humble yourself before your God, your request has been heard in heaven. I have come in answer to your prayer, but for twenty-one days the spirit prince of the kingdom of Persia blocked my way. Then Michael, one of the archangels, came to help me and I left him there with the spirit prince of the kingdom of Persia. Now I am here to explain what will happen to your people in the future, for the vision concerns a time yet to come." Daniel 10:12-15.* (NLT) We must not give up praying, even when we don't see the answers coming immediately. Our prayers are being heard and moving the heavens. Daniel had decided to fast meat, wine, rich foods and wore no fragrant lotions, and the Lord honored his prayers with the answer he was seeking. Ephesians 6:18 tells us to *"pray in the Spirit at all times and on every* occasion. *Stay alert and be persistent in your prayers for all believers everywhere.*" (NLT)

Read His word. I expect to be filled with all the good things of God, while I read His word. And what I don't understand now, I will later. He is the living water and the bread of life. His word tells me that man will not live by bread alone but by every word that proceeds from His mouth. (See Matt 4:4) In John 5:39 Jesus is speaking to Jewish leaders and tells them that scriptures point to Him. How will we know Him, if we don't go to the Word that tells us who He is? *Song of Solomon 1:2 Kiss me with the kisses of your mouth…* (ESV) His mouth is His word. When I am kissed with the Word, my heart starts to beat fast and I am so excited to hear what He wants to tell me. He opens up the windows of my understanding so I can breathe in His word and let it bring healing to my mind and body and restoration for my soul. I feel special because the God of the universe decided to take some time to spend with me and tell me things that woo me to come closer. *Psalm 27:7-8 ⁷…Be merciful and answer me! ⁸ My heart has heard you say, "Come and talk with me." And my heart responds, "Lord, I am coming."* (NLT)

Journal what He tells you. It's always been a habit of mine that when I open my Bible, I have my journal and pen ready. During times of fasting the Lord passes on to us so much information. Some of it will make sense immediately, and some of it will be scriptures for a future day. Journaling keeps these scriptures for us to be encouraged and to look back on for clarity when we hit foggy paths on our journey. Some of those things we underlined or jotted down in our journals or notebooks will be there for a future time when missing pieces need to be added to an unfinished puzzle in our life. Our journals will be a road map for the plans He has for our lives. We won't understand those paths all at once, so we will pull our road map out each time we get confused or lost and then find ourselves getting back on the right path. And, each time we find our way again, we feel restored and safe. *Psalm 23:2-3 ²He makes me lie down in green pastures; He leads me beside quiet waters. ³He restores my soul; He guides me in the paths of righteousness For His name's sake.* (NASB) *Psalm 5:8 O Lord, lead me in Your righteousness because of my foes; Make Your way straight before me.* (NASB)

Journaling helps us file our thoughts so we can move on and be able to receive more information, revelation, wisdom and knowledge. If I know I wrote it down, my thoughts don't have to stay in one place. I can keep seeking and come back to it another time. There are times we are emotionally struggling with issues in our lives, and our thinking isn't real clear. As long as I keep journaling, when my head is clear, I know I can go back and retrieve what I have written and continue in the direction the Lord wants me to take.

Be satisfied with the meal He serves you. *Psalm 81:10 For it was I, the Lord your God, who rescued you from the land of Egypt. Open your mouth wide, and I will fill it with good things.* (NLT) Sometimes our expectations are greater than what we received at that time, and there might be a tendency to feel like we failed or wasted our time. The fact is: our expectations were met, but they were met by God in a way that He felt we were ready to receive. He knows what we need and how much we can handle at one time. I find it to be very exciting because it leaves me wanting more. Another scripture God gave me was *Psalm 92:10 But you have exalted my horn like that of the wild ox; you have poured over me fresh oil.* (ESV) In the scripture the horn is employed as a symbol of strength and power. Anointing the head with oil signifies joy, contentment, and satisfaction. Throughout my journey with fasting the Lord showed me that He was walking with me, feeding, protecting, and comforting me even when dark times came and would come in the future. I felt joy, contentment and **satisfaction** knowing He was in charge.

Pray, read His word, journal and be satisfied with the meal He serves you. This is the best time since your mind is clear and ready to receive.

Questions to Ponder from Chapter Five

1. Do you journal? If so, how long have you journaled, and why is it important to you?

2. When is the last time you've gone back and read your journals from the past?

3. If you don't journal, how do you keep track of the things that God shows you?

4. Take some time to go back and read some things you have journaled in the last month or underlined in your Bible. Did anything stand out that you might have forgotten?

CHAPTER SIX

The fourth key to successful fasting for spiritual breakthrough: **Make yourself accountable to those you know who will help you succeed.**

Fasting Day Four

On my fourth day I was doing really well, but I perceived that it was because I maintained my excitement and still had great expectations. My mouth was still wide open waiting to be filled with more of Him. I felt great peace.

It's important that we don't wear our fasting for others to see in order to look holy and spiritual. We also need to be wary of playing the role of the victim so others will pity us. Fasting should be done in secret. The right hand should not know what the left hand is doing, except when we share with a few people for **accountability**. This will help us stay on track, give people a chance to pray for us and encourage us when we feel weak. *Psalm 37:30-31 ³⁰The godly offer good counsel; they teach right from wrong. ³¹ They have made God's law their own, so they will never slip from his path.* (NLT) I surround myself with other people who practice fasting and are prayer intercessors; because I know they understand what I'm going through. Intercessors will pray about it, and if the Lord gives them a word of encouragement or correction, they will share it with me. The more I am in the Word, I will find the confirmation is usually what I have already been reading and receiving.

While fasting it is important that we never underestimate the opposition from the enemy. We can read about opposition in the following scriptures:

1. Job 1-2 - Satan and Job - Job was a man who feared God and avoided evil. He was the richest man in the area. God was talking to Satan one day and asked him if he had noticed Job and how Job was a fearless man. Satan told him if everything was taken away from him, he would curse God. So God let Satan test Job. He lost his family, protection, wealth, and health. The only thing Satan couldn't do to him was take

his life. Although he endured great suffering, he remained faithful to God, and God doubled what he had lost.

2. Matthew 4:1-11 - Satan and Jesus - Jesus is led into the wilderness to be tempted by Satan. (Read in Chapter One of this book)

3. Mark 4:1-20 - Satan and the seed that was sown – Jesus told a parable about a farmer sowing seed, and what the results were for each area where the seed fell. The seed was God's word, and when the farmer dropped seed on the footpath, Satan came immediately, and took it away.

4. Luke 22:1-6 - Satan and Judas – Because Judas was corrupt; Satan was able to enter Judas, who left and betrayed Jesus for thirty pieces of silver. When Judas realized he had betrayed an innocent man, he was filled with remorse. Then he went and hung himself.

5. Luke 22:31-32 - Satan and Peter - Satan asked permission to "sift Peter like wheat." Peter was the strong leader-type of the disciples so Satan's sifting came in the form of weakening him in front of others. This happened when he denied Jesus three times as He had foretold. Peter was a broken man and left the scene weeping bitterly. (He did not stay this way, and you can see his transformation in the book of Acts.)

6. Revelation 2:10 - Satan and the saints of God - Jesus tells the Church of Smyrna that the devil was going to throw some of the saints into prison to "test" them. They would suffer for ten days and were encouraged to remain faithful even in the face of death.

The battle between the flesh and spirit will be intensified while fasting, but God gives us His instructions on how to withstand the battle. First we need to recognize who we are fighting. *Ephesians 6:12 For we are not fighting against flesh-and-blood enemies, but against evil rulers and authorities of the unseen world, against mighty powers in this dark world, and against evil spirits in the heavenly places.* (NLT) Next, we need to be humble and resist the devil and his temptations. *James 4:7 So humble yourselves before God. Resist the devil, and he will flee from you.* (NLT) Finally, we need to stay alert. *I Peter 5:8-9 [8]Stay alert! Watch out for your great enemy, the devil. He prowls around like a roaring lion, looking for someone to devour. [9]Stand firm against him, and be strong in your faith...*(NLT)

This battle will include:

1. **Pride:**

    Proverbs 16:18 Pride goes before destruction and haughtiness before a fall. (NLT)

Proverbs 11:2 Pride leads to disgrace but with humility comes wisdom. (NLT)

It's very easy to fall into the, "I'm holier than you" trap when you fast. Remember we are doing this to **humble ourselves**, not lift ourselves up. We don't want most people to know what we are doing. This is between God and us.

2. **Jealousy and selfishness:**

   James 3:14-15 But if you are bitterly jealous and there is selfish ambition in your heart, don't cover up the truth with boasting and lying. ¹⁵ For jealousy and selfishness are not God's kind of wisdom. Such things are earthly, unspiritual, and demonic. (NLT) Jealousy shows its ugly head, when we start wanting what everyone else has and become discontent with our lives and with what God has already given us. We can do this with spiritual gifts as well. We all have a special mission to fulfill in the body of Christ, and we complement each other, because we are not all functioning the same way.

3. **Power, Protection and Provision:**

   Matthew 4 This was discussed in detail in Chapter One of this book.

4. **Anger :**

Ephesians 4:26-27 And *"don't sin by letting anger control you"*
Don't let the sun go down while you are still angry, ²⁷ for anger
gives a foothold to the devil. (NLT)

When we are fasting, we get weak. Our tempers can erupt at the simplest things. We have to remember, though, that what spills out when we are bumped, is the very thing that God may be trying to refine. And even though we may have been fasting for a different reason, the answer He will provide will come in different ways and could meet needs we didn't realize we had.

The enemy is threatened when we fast, because fasting exposes his plans, and how much control we have let him have in our lives. Our idols are exposed, and we can no longer live in a state of denial. Making ourselves accountable to those who will help us succeed lessens the influence the enemy has over us. They will advise, encourage and pray.

Before going into a fast ask God to show you who will help you succeed, and have them start praying immediately. Don't wait until the fast begins, because the moment you think about fasting, the warfare begins.

If you regularly fast at least once or twice a week, it is so important to ask the Lord for help before each fasting day. Don't assume you can do this in your own strength. The enemy will use the above examples to thwart your plans. I have to pray every week that He will help me make it and not yield to temptations for each day I fast. Just because I was successful last week, does not mean I won't struggle this week. Every fasting day is different.

Having people pray for us and seeking their counsel will help us remember, we are not alone, and strength comes in numbers.

Questions to Ponder from Chapter Six

1. Can you think of any time in recent weeks when having someone keep you accountable kept you from making a big mistake? What did it protect you from?

2. What are some reasons to have an accountability partner?

3. What are some things in your life that you should be making yourself accountable for to someone close that you can trust?

4. What attitudes could pop up while you are fasting?

5. What are some ways the enemy has intensified the battle between your flesh and spirit?

6. What other biblical examples can you think of where the enemy caused problems with a biblical character? What methods did he use?

7. What are some idols you have been tempted with that are filling a void that only God can fill?

8. Read Isaiah 29:13. What is false worship?

9. Make sure to contact your support team and share your answers to the battles you are facing so they can pray for you.

CHAPTER SEVEN

***The fifth key to successful fasting for
spiritual breakthrough:* Let God's word
penetrate deep into your heart, and apply
what you've learned to your life.**

Fasting Day Five

Day five and I felt great! I had hunger pangs, but they were a reminder of how I needed God to fill me with Himself and His word. I was having a love affair with His word. That morning as I was getting ready to start my day, He showed me how His word was fruit, and as it grows in me it gives off seed that will be sown in due season. I did not receive any specific direction from the Lord on this fifth day, but I saw myself in a place of preparation, and I was overwhelmed with joy and anticipation.

Read, meditate, and make a plan to turn knowledge gained into experience and application. During your fast God will begin giving you revelations. It's so important to not lose these truths or leave them on a shelf somewhere. Read them over and over, and give a lot of thought and attention to them. Let it soak in so that you can take what you have learned and apply it to your everyday life. *Proverbs 4:20-21 ²⁰My child pay attention to what I say. Listen carefully to my words ²¹... **Let them penetrate deep into your heart** for they bring life to those who find them.* (NLT)

I found myself continually reading and rereading all He had given me, and I got more and more understanding. This caused me to become more excited, as I started to live out His word from my understanding. *Proverbs 4:25-27 ²⁵Look straight ahead, and fix your eyes on what lies before you. ²⁶ Mark out a straight path for your feet; stay on the safe path. ²⁷Don't get sidetracked; keep your feet from following evil* (NLT) We need to keep reading the Word to receive understanding from the Word to reveal what that straight path is. We will become more aware of the traps that sidetrack us, and we will either avoid them or take them out of our lives completely.

Sometimes when God's word penetrates deep into our heart, God will bring to mind those we need to reconcile with. *Matthew 5:23-24 ²³So if you are presenting a sacrifice at the altar in the Temple and you suddenly remember that someone has something against you,*

[24] *Leave your sacrifice there at the altar. Go and be reconciled to that person. Then come and offer your sacrifice to God.* (NLT) Pray for opportunities to make things right, so the enemy can't come with his pointed finger and accuse you or the one you have offended. We need clean hands and a pure heart to ascend the high places God has prepared for us. (See Psalm 24:3-4) *If you sincerely try to make things right and your offender does not forgive, you will still be set free.*

There was a time in my life, when I had offended two of my closet friends and another girl on my Women's Ministry Council. No matter how hard I tried to make things right, my two friends just wouldn't forgive me. They would say they did, but would totally ignore me when I got to church. It hurt so badly. I truly wanted reconciliation and was willing to take the blame, but forgiveness didn't come and although it hurt, I knew that I had done everything right even going so far as to getting my pastor to mediate for me. The third girl and I did reconcile and were able to move forward. As far as I know I never did get forgiven by one of my friends. I lost total contact with her. I moved to another city and moved on in my life. About two years later the second friend called me. I was shocked but so happy to hear from her. And even though our conversation didn't go the way I had hoped, she did forgive me then. I was hoping for a restored friendship, but that was not going to happen. I was grateful for the closure though. It felt so good to be forgiven.

Refuse to obey the flesh. When God's word penetrates deeply, we no longer want to disobey. *Romans 12:1-2 ¹And so, dear brothers and sisters, I plead with you to give your bodies to God because of all he has done for you. Let them be a living and holy sacrifice—the kind he will find acceptable. This is truly the way to worship him ² Don't copy the behavior and customs of this world, but let God transform you into a new person by changing the way you think. Then you will learn to know God's will for you, which is good and pleasing and perfect.* (NLT)

As we receive new revelations, and we experience a deeper intimacy with the Lord, we start recognizing things in our lives that need to change. Our heart longs desperately to please the Lord and bring joy to Him with our actions. This is the time to commit these changes to the Lord. We may not be able to change everything that is revealed at once. But we can ask the Lord to help us take one step at a time. He is still working on us, and He is faithful to complete what He has started. (See Philippians 1:6) He patiently waits for us to be ready and willing.

Let God's word penetrate deep into your heart, so you can apply changes, make restitution, and have victory over your fleshly desires.

Questions to Ponder from Chapter Seven

1. What is it today that has sidetracked you from spending time with our Lord?

2. What does your devotional time look like?

3. What is your definition of meditating?

4. What scripture has the Lord given you lately that you have been meditating on? What has He been revealing in the meditation process?

5. Has the Holy Spirit asked you to make restitution with anyone and have you followed through?

6. What is the biggest fight you are having with the flesh right now?

7. What is the latest application of His word that you have seen taking place in your life most recently?

CHAPTER EIGHT

The sixth key to successful fasting for spiritual breakthrough: **Become familiar with the needs of your city.**

Fasting Day Six

D way six was rough, but I remained strong and optimistic. At 1:00 AM I woke up with a start. I thought I heard a piercing child's scream in my neighborhood. I walked around inside my house several times and looked out windows, and concluded I had imagined it. But I felt so compelled to pray for my neighbors and anyone around here, who might be in trouble. Then the Lord brought to mind many people, and I remember praying until I fell asleep. I remembered after waking up from a deep sleep, praying for one person in particular, but

I know I prayed for other people for several hours. When I fell back to sleep, I was tormented in my dreams.

I had a very intense dream the night before, that was very detailed. It was one of the strangest dreams I'd had in a long time, and it totally wiped me out for the whole day. The only reason I share this is that you may have strange dreams too and this is very normal. The mind can be very detailed in dreams while fasting. I felt like I had been watching a screen play for a movie. Although the intensity of it drained me of energy, I did not lose my anticipation.

Day six of my fast the Lord encouraged me with *Psalm 145:15-16* *¹⁵The eyes of all look to you in hope; you give them their food as they need it. ¹⁶ When you open your hand, you satisfy the hunger and thirst of every living thing.* (NLT) I realized that no amount of food could match what God had been giving me in His word. My heart was leaping with great joy. He was giving me so much in the Word that I felt like I was going to burst wide open.

This particular day was a bread and water day only. My daughter Meghan was fasting with me, so I made fresh bread for both of us. The hardest thing I was discovering about fasting was that I couldn't always sit with my Bible or stop and pray at all meal times. My schedule kept me moving from one thing to another. I did carry my Bible and notebooks and journal with me everywhere I went, and every time I had an opportunity, I was in the Word and waiting with expectation for what He was going to give me for that day.

With this key God was showing me to pray and ask where He would use me as a vessel that brings life to my city. We start by praying for peace and for God to reveal the needs of people within our city. How do we affect people's lives if we don't know their needs? How do we become a unified city if we aren't praying for peace and prosperity within her walls? We go through the city to get to the church, because the church is in the midst of her. We can't turn a blind eye to the needs in the city and expect the church to move in the power of God. *Psalm 122:1-4 ¹I was glad when they said to me, "Let us go to the house of the Lord." ² And now here we are, standing inside your gates, O Jerusalem. ³ Jerusalem is a well-built city; its seamless walls cannot be breached. ⁴ All the tribes of Israel—the Lord's people— make their pilgrimage here. They come to give thanks to the name of the Lord...* (NLT) The key word is glad. It's an attitude thing. Why do we go to church? Is it because it's tradition? Is it because we have to? Is it "the thing to do"? Do we complain? NO! We look forward to it, or at least we should. Verse 3-4 tells us when we come to the house of God; we are knit together as one unit to give thanks to the name of the Lord. Verses 6-8 talks about praying for the peace and prosperity in the city, where the house of the Lord is situated. And verse 9 says, *"For the sake of the house of the Lord our God, I will seek what is best for you O Jerusalem.*" (NLT) (Replace Jerusalem with the name of your city to make it more personal.)

It is vital that we seek out what is best for our city, if we want to be an effective Christ follower and an effective and powerful church. How easy it is to get so comfortable in our churches or gatherings that the only place we look is inside our own walls. We need to be looking around our city for ways to affect it for the glory of God.

As our prayer for others intensifies, God allows us to get inside of a person's heart, so we can sense their pain, confusion, and suffering. Their pain becomes my pain, ***and my pain becomes my prayer.*** You wrestle through it for them before the presence of God, so that they may be set free. You invest a part of yourself into their situation, and their suffering then becomes personal to you.

When we are fasting, we need to not only remember to pray for peace in our city, but we need to take the answers God gives us in response to these prayers and implement them. How exciting it would be to be fasting, praying, and seeking God and then hear that a church down the street is breaking out in revival. Or hear that God broke loose in a city council meeting, find out that someone was miraculously healed or that the homeless were finding shelter not only physically but shelter under the wings of the most high God. We can't even begin to understand what God can do with one person's prayer through fasting and seeking him.

At the writing of this book we were feeding the less fortunate and homeless on Monday evenings in our church. In the beginning I felt so overwhelmed with all the struggles they were facing, the addictions they were dealing with, and the lack of salvation in their lives. I felt like such an insignificant person with little means to make their lives better, so I avoided having conversations with them, because I didn't have any answers and couldn't fix them or their situations. Then one day my husband came into my office and asked me if I had some spare candles I could give a woman who was coming on Monday nights. I had a bunch given to me for our 24 Hour Prayer Focus so I said, "Sure send her in." When Jennifer (not her real name) came to pick up the candles, and I saw and felt her gratitude at such a small offering, I realized that the smallest of gestures are sometimes the most important. I gained such a tender heart toward her and feel as if the Lord has placed her under my wing of prayer. I have such a love for her and I know it's God's love for her working through me. It was during a Daniel fast, that the Lord revealed this to me.

Every Wednesday from 4-6 our Prayer Room intercedes for our city, its officials, schools, other churches in our community and the unsaved. Several people in our church have decided to use this day as a weekly fast. I can't wait to hear and see how God is going to change our city through these times of fasting, seeking and praying. I have total faith and confidence that He is already moving.

Questions to Ponder from Chapter Eight

1. If you know you are going to have a busy day, what things could you do in advance to allow yourself time in the Word and/or time for prayer?

2. Why is it important to serve outside your church?

3. Do you know what the needs are of your city are?

4. Do you know the needs of your city? What could you do to start seeking what's best for your city?

5. List some things in your city that you could involve yourself with that are not related to your church needs?

6. What kind of community service projects have you done in the past? Currently?

7. When was the last time you reached out to help someone who was in need and not in your church? What did you do? How did it impact the person you helped?

CHAPTER NINE

The seventh key to successful spiritual fasting: **Share! Share! Share! Share what God is doing and celebrate!**

Fasting Day Seven

Day seven I found myself hit with "The Blues." The day before, I had watched two baseball coaches totally mistreat my son and make him feel worthless. I felt the Lord tell me to hold my tongue, that there were things my boy had to learn from this, so I prayed for them to see his value and for him to know he was valuable regardless of whether they saw it or not. I was so miserable for him; I felt like crying, but I held it all in. I didn't want to be consumed with bitterness. I went so far as to write the editor of the newspaper, and even though I didn't mention any names, I never sent it. I think it was just a way God designed for me to get it off my chest! I was learning there were some things you share and some things you don't.

The Lord was faithful to continue to feed me from His word; even though my soul was so downcast, and even in my sadness I had an inner joy. Psalm 63:2 says that when we are in the house of God, we should be able to gaze upon His power and His glory. Verse *5 say: You satisfy me more than the richest feast...* (NLT) God was still giving me so much through prayer and His word. It was truly better than the most chocolate of candy bars. I could have been eating candy in my sadness and normally would have in other circumstances, but this day I was letting His word feed me. *Verse 6 says: I lie awake thinking of you, meditating on you through the night.* (NLT) I found myself constantly in prayer or thinking about His word, and how much He had opened it up in me. I was falling more and more in love with Him.

Share! Share! Share what God is doing in your life! There might be one person just waiting for some word of encouragement, warning or confirmation. We are told in Hebrews to stir one another on to good deeds. (See Hebrew 10:24-25) and in the Psalms we are told to tell of His greatness. *Psalm 145:6-7. 10-12 ⁶Your awe-inspiring deeds will be on every tongue; I will proclaim your greatness. ⁷Everyone will share the story of your wonderful goodness; they will sing with joy* *about your righteousness. ¹⁰All of your works will thank you, LORD, and your faithful followers will praise you. ¹¹They will talk together about the glory of your kingdoms; they will celebrate examples of your power. ¹² They will tell about your mighty deeds and about the majesty and glory of your reign.* (NLT) What God gives us in times of fasting will not only impact our lives, but it will inspire obedience in others. How can we not share what He is doing in our own lives knowing that by our testimony He is saving others? David, being a man after God's own heart, shared constantly in the Psalms about how great God was to him, and what He was doing in his life. Today, his words are still encouraging those who read them, and their lives are being changed.

My husband was inspired to fast and pray through one of our 24 Hour Prayer Focuses. What happened to him not only changed his life, but changed our church. As he shared with others what God was doing in his life through fasting, some of the members of our church decided to see what God would do in their lives as they too fasted. Because of my husband's obedience we had a prayer and fasting team at our church. There were people praying and fasting for our church for every day of the week, 24 hours a day.

One day Greg asked me what I had done with the notes and journal about fasting with the nine spiritual keys. As he read them he encouraged me to put this in a book. We have been using this book as a bible study in our small group and every person who is a part of our group has been inspired to make fasting a part of their life. A brand new Christian in our church, after reading my book decided to give fasting a try and was set free from smoking and he wasn't even fasting for that reason. He not only quit smoking but he felt and incredible intimacy begin in his life with our Lord. In my own life fasting has become an important part of my lifestyle. It's no longer something I do once in a while.

All of this came about because someone decided to **share, share, share** what God was doing in their life and stirred another on to "good things."

Questions to Ponder from Chapter Nine

1. Why is it important to share what God is doing or has done through your fast?

2. Name at least three things that sharing your story will do for another person.

3. Read Psalm 105:1-6. Who are we supposed to tell about what He has done?

4. Read Psalm 107:2. What are you supposed to tell others?

5. What was the last thing you shared about what the Lord had done in your life? How did it make the person or persons you shared it with feel?

CHAPTER TEN

The eighth key to successful spiritual fasting: **Continue to seek wisdom daily, even as the fast comes to an end.**

Fasting Day Eight

One thing that kept going through my mind over and over was, if we are just fasting without prayer and seeking His face through His word, it's not going to meet our expectations. Before we even begin our fast, we need to know that we are seeking only Him, and in that process and love relationship He will reveal things to us. When we speak of fasting, praying and seeking God through His word should follow. Otherwise I wonder what are we fasting for?

It would be very easy to come out of fasting with a full heart and many revelations. The danger that follows is; that we will quit seeking. Praying and seeking God should never end when the fast does. *Proverbs 8:34-35* ³⁴*Joyful are those who listen to me, watching for me daily at my gates, waiting for me outside my home!* ³⁵ *For whoever finds me finds life and receives favor from the* LORD. (NLT) If we quit seeking wisdom, we will bring injury to ourselves. Wisdom offers many benefits. Read the book of Proverbs and learn what they are.

Here are just a few of the benefits of wisdom:

1. Gives us common sense
2. Gives us understanding
3. Has excellent things to tell us
4. Is truth
5. Gives wholesome and good advice
6. Is plain and clear to those who want to learn
7. More valuable than material possessions
8. Discerns knowledge and gives discernment
9. Gives good advice and success
10. Gives insight and strength
11. Gives wealth
12. Was God's constant delight, rejoicing always in His presence
13. Brings happiness

14. Brings life

15. Wins approval from the Lord

It used to be, when I fasted there were many years in-between those times. Today I have realized, I can't continue receiving from the Lord the way He desires to give, if I don't make it a lifestyle. I know I will fast at least one day a week, but I take it now one day, one week, one month at a time as to what those fasts will be and how long He wants me to stay on it. I stay yielded to the fast God wants me on. But, as I wait for Him to lead, I have chosen to live the fasting lifestyle at least weekly, because I want more. I am hungry and ready to go as far as God wants to take me.

My prayer is; that my Father would help me continuously look for wisdom and not to seek my own counsel. I want to be able to be a blessing to others and impact their lives, so they will draw closer to Him, as they see His light shining through me. I want the light of His countenance to shine on me, and I want to feel it. I asked the Lord to search me and know my heart, test me and know my thoughts. I want Him to point out anything that offends Him, and that He would lead me along the path of everlasting life. (See Psalm 139)

As we go through times of fasting, prayer and seeking, we allow God to reveal His heart to us, and then we begin to see what is offensive in our lives. We are more receptive to the change He wants to make in our lives, so that we can draw closer and understand His heart for us. He adores us. In Song of Solomon when we gaze at Him, we capture His heart, and His heart beats fast for us, His beloved. (See Song of Solomon 4:9 NLT and NASB)

Don't stop seeking God's heart. He longs for us to run to the secret places with Him. He longs to tell us how He feels about us. He longs for us to fall crazy deep in love with Him the way He has fallen for us. And, when we understand and receive this, we will love ourselves and pour that love out on others as the first and second New Testament Commandments tell us. (See Matthew 22:37-40)

Questions to Ponder from Chapter Ten

1. What should we be doing when we fast?

2. What is the danger we face when the fast is over?

3. What will happen if we quit seeking wisdom?

4. What would the fasting lifestyle look like for you?

5. What are some things that God will reveal to us about ourselves during time of fasting?

6. If you have fasted before what were some of the things that God revealed to you about yourself?

7. What are the First and Second New Testament Commandments, and how can we know that we are obeying them?

CHAPTER ELEVEN

The ninth key to successful fasting for spiritual breakthrough: **Remember the fast is just the beginning: There's more to come!**

Fasting Day Nine

Day Nine brought many more revelations. I was doing very well physically and spiritually. Mentally I was a bit down, but it was just dealing with the everyday ups and downs. I never lost my sense of purpose and was still looking to the future with hope and optimism.

Jeremiah 29:11-14 For I know the plans I have for you," says the Lord. "They are plans for good and not for disaster, to give you a future and a hope. ¹² In those days when you pray, I will listen. ¹³ If you look for me wholeheartedly, you will find me. ¹⁴ *I will be found by you," says the Lord. "I will end your captivity and restore your fortunes.* (NLT)

How many things in life hold us captive? What are the hardest things to go without... food, TV, computer, music, cigarettes, bitterness, alcohol, drugs, pornography, selfishness, and the list goes on. My stomach during the fast was telling me it's food. But, I knew there were other things that I was not even aware of that the Lord was going to reveal to me. As I sought Him earnestly, I found Him, and He did end my captivity to a lot of things. God gave me a promise, and He fulfilled it. My desire today remains the same; I still don't want to be held captive by the flesh. The more I fast, pray and seek the Lord, the more He reveals, and the more I am set free. I only want to be satisfied by the things the Lord gives to me.

Mark 14:38 Keep watch and pray, so you will not give in to temptation. For the spirit is willing, but the body is weak. (NLT) Without prayer, and when our focus is off God, we will give in to temptation. I think fasting helps clear our heads so we can stay alert.

The Lord was faithful and gave me what He said He would if I was obedient. He gave me nine keys to successful fasting for spiritual breakthrough. The conference was amazing. God used my journey with Him to encourage the women to fast, pray and seek God. Every once in a while, I will run into a woman from that conference, and she will tell me how my story impacted her life and opened doors to fasting that she too had disregarded.

Fasting is just the beginning but what comes after will change the course of history for you and those God has chosen to put in your path. There is so much to learn about God, and I'm convinced when we step into heaven, we are going to find that "we've only just begun..."

Questions to Ponder from Chapter Eleven

1. What do you find in your life that you are held captive by?

2. What do you find most lacking in your life right now that fasting could bring to you from the father?

3. Take some time to seek the Father and ask when He would like you to join Him in a time of fasting, praying and seeking His face.

CHAPTER TWELVE

Conclusion

G od was true to His word to me and had given me what He promised. I had my Nine Keys, but I knew that there was more in store for me personally. Some of the questions I was anticipating answers from Him were: What will You be teaching me? What more will I find out about myself? What will I need to change? Whose life will I have the privilege of impacting for the better? How much closer will I be to You? Will I be wiser?

I continued my fast after God gave me the Nine Keys. Although my ninth day was hard due to extreme hunger and a headache, I pressed forward. I was reading a book (I don't remember which one) on fasting that informed me that the "blahs" were not uncommon during this time. I didn't like that feeling, but at least I felt "normal".

It was on my 12th day, I had my first temptation to cheat. I was able to overcome, but I was left with this thought: With fasting comes pain in the head and stomach, dizziness, cravings etc…but, as we overcome these physical sensations, we realize, there is no other temptation we will not be able to overcome. Because I have felt pain, the blahs, temptations through hunger, I know it's not any different from other temptations that will come along. The ability to overcome gave me a new strength, tremendous excitement and closeness to the Lord. *Isaiah 40:31 But those who trust in the Lord will find **new** strength. They will soar high on wings like eagles. They will run and not grow weary. They will walk and not faint.* (NLT)

I went into fasting believing, that I was going to hear from God, He was going to change my life, and I would impact others, and I was not disappointed. I opened my mouth wide, and God filled it! I was more satisfied with the feast He provided in His word, than I was with real food. Don't get me wrong, because I still love the taste of food, and I savor every bite, but I realized the amount of time I spend preparing and eating had been spent on praying and seeking, and I was so full. I am so grateful, that God took me on that journey.

My hope and prayer for you, as you have read this is; that you will be inspired to take your own journey into fasting, He will give you the desires of your heart, and you will be empowered in your relationship with Him and others.

So in conclusion I remind you once more: the **Nine Keys to Successful Fasting for Spiritual Breakthrough** are:

1. Go into fasting wholeheartedly and with an attitude of great expectation.

2. Know your purpose and what type of fast you are going to do. Make a plan!!

3. Pray, Read His word, Journal what He tells you, and be satisfied with the meal He provides.

4. Make yourself accountable to those you know who will help you succeed.

5. Let God's word penetrate deep into your heart and apply what you've learned to your life.

6. Become familiar with the needs of your City.

7. Share! Share! Share! Share what God is doing and celebrate!

8. Continue to seek wisdom daily, even when the fast comes to an end.

9. Remember the fast is just the beginning: There's more to come.

Printed in the United States
By Bookmasters